This Is  W9-CEK-456

Draw a picture of yourself here. Then circle the first letter of your name.

A B C D E F G H I J K L M
N O P Q R S T U V W X Y Z

Spring Flowers

Cut each line from the bottom of the page to the top of each flower stem.

How many bees do you see?

3

Summer Safari

Help each baby animal find its parent. Cut each line from the left all the way to the parent.

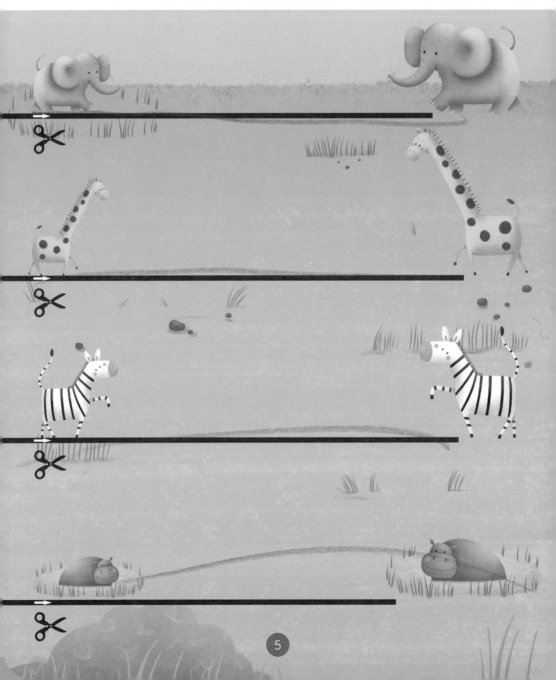

Fall Flyers

Cut along the lines to help each bird get home.

Winter Riders

Cut along the lines to show each snowboarder how to ride down the hill.

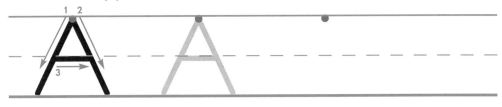

A a This is an uppercase **A**.
This is a lowercase **a**.

Trace the uppercase **A**. Then write your own.

A A A

Trace the lowercase **a**. Then write your own.

a a a

Now trace **A** and **a** to finish the sentence.

Andy eats
ants.

11

Awesome!

Find and circle the **8** objects that begin with the letter a in this Hidden Pictures puzzle.

ant   arrow   acorn   artist's brush   ax   apricot   apple   airplane

Trace the uppercase **B**. Then write your own.

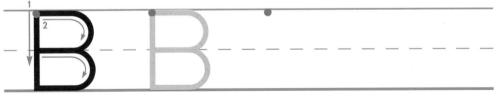

Trace the lowercase **b**. Then write your own.

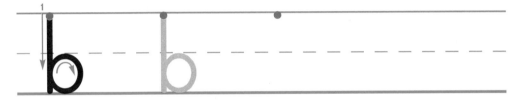

Now trace **B** and **b** to finish the sentence.

Bella builds
with blocks.

Bob's Bakery

Circle each **B** you see. How many did you find?

What else do you see that starts with **B?**

This is an uppercase C.
This is a lowercase c.

Trace the uppercase C. Then write your own.

Trace the lowercase c. Then write your own.

Now trace C and c to finish the sentence.

Cora craves

cupcakes.

C Is for Cat!

Circle the differences you see between these pictures of cuddly cats.

Can you think of 3 words that rhyme with *cat*?

Dd

This is an uppercase **D**.
This is a lowercase **d**.

Trace the uppercase **D**. Then write your own.

D D

Trace the lowercase **d**. Then write your own.

d d

Now trace **D** and **d** to finish the sentence.

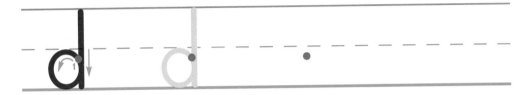

Donald dives

deep.

Dog Daycare

Follow the D's to help Dexter meet up with his friends.

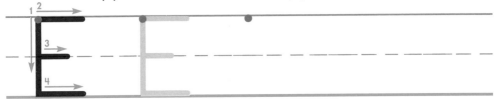

E e This is an uppercase E.
This is a lowercase e.

Trace the uppercase E. Then write your own.

E E

Trace the lowercase e. Then write your own.

e e

Now trace E and e to finish the sentence.

Eve gathers

eggs.

Count and circle 4 eggs.

Elephant Eve

Find and circle the **6** objects that start with the letter e in this excellent Hidden Pictures puzzle.

éclair

eggplant

engine

earthworm

egg

earmuffs

Ff

This is an uppercase **F**.
This is a lowercase **f**.

Trace the uppercase **F**. Then write your own.

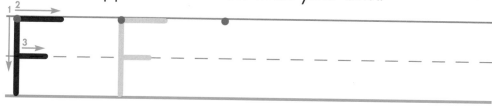

Trace the lowercase **f**. Then write your own.

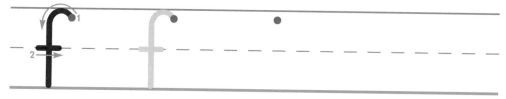

Now trace **F** and **f** to finish the sentence.

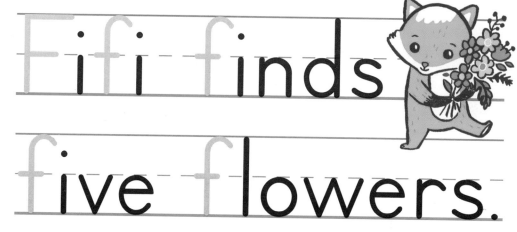

Fifi finds five flowers.

F Is for Fish!

Draw a line from each fish to its match.

What else can you think of that starts with the letter F?

Gg This is an uppercase G.
This is a lowercase g.

Trace the uppercase G. Then write your own.

Trace the lowercase g. Then write your own.

Now trace G and g to finish the sentence.

Gary and
Gail giggle.

35

Great Green Goblins

Circle each G you see. How many did you find?

Hh
This is an uppercase **H**.
This is a lowercase **h**.

Trace the uppercase **H**. Then write your own.

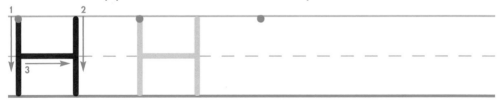

Trace the lowercase **h**. Then write your own.

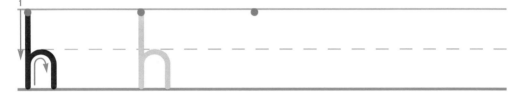

Now trace **H** and **h** to finish the sentence.

Hedgehogs

hop happily.

Have a Hamburger?

Find and circle the **10** objects that start with the letter **h** in this Hidden Pictures puzzle.

hook

hard hat

horseshoe

hatchet

harmonica

harp

honeybee

hare

handsaw

hammer

41

I i   This is an uppercase I.
This is a lowercase i.

Trace the uppercase I. Then write your own.

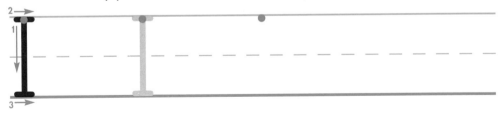

Trace the lowercase i. Then write your own.

Now trace I and i to finish the sentence.

Irvin inspects
insects.

43

Ice Time

Follow the I's to help Ivan and Irene skate to their dad.

FINISH

START

45

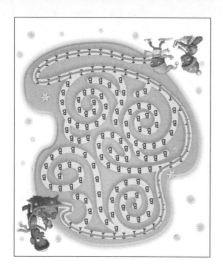

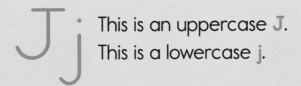

J j : This is an uppercase **J**.
This is a lowercase **j**.

Trace the uppercase **J**. Then write your own.

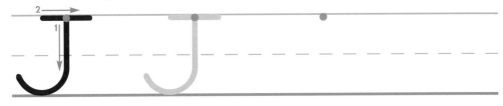

Trace the lowercase **j**. Then write your own.

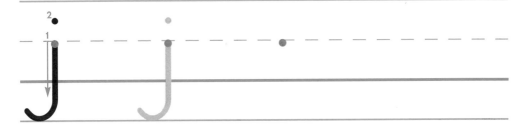

Now trace **J** and **j** to finish the sentence.

Jane juggles joyfully.

47

J Is for Jump!

Jump on in, and circle every silly thing you see.

Can you think of another word that starts with the letter J?

49

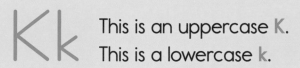

This is an uppercase **K**.
This is a lowercase **k**.

Trace the uppercase **K**. Then write your own.

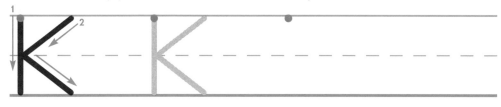

Trace the lowercase **k**. Then write your own.

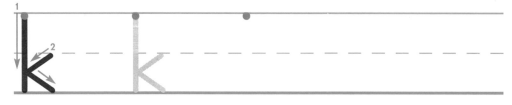

Now trace **K** and **k** to finish the sentence.

Kiko flies
a kite.

51

Kid Karaoke

Find and circle the **7** objects that start with the letter k in this Hidden Pictures puzzle.

ketchup

kazoo

kangaroo

kayak

key

kite

koala

53

L l This is an uppercase L.
This is a lowercase l.

Trace the uppercase L. Then write your own.

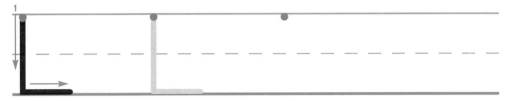

Trace the lowercase l. Then write your own.

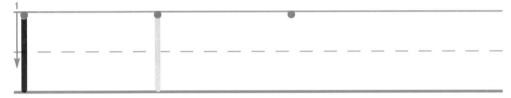

Now trace L and l to finish the sentence.

Leroy folds laundry.

Leo Likes Lions

Circle each L you see. How many did you find?

Can you think of another animal that starts with the letter L?

M m

This is an uppercase **M**.
This is a lowercase **m**.

Trace the uppercase **M**. Then write your own.

Trace the lowercase **m**. Then write your own.

Now trace **M** and **m** to finish the sentence.

Monster Max

smiles.

M Is for Mermaid!

Circle the differences you see between these pictures of merry mermaids.

Can you think of 2 other words that begin with the letter M?

Trace the uppercase N. Then write your own.

N N

Trace the lowercase n. Then write your own.

n n

Now trace N and n to finish the sentence.

Nancy counts
nine nuts.

Nest Rest

Follow the **N**'s to help Neko reach her nest.

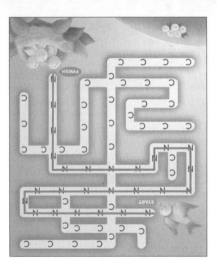

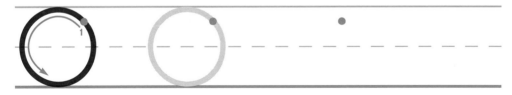

This is an uppercase O.
This is a lowercase o.

Trace the uppercase O. Then write your own.

Trace the lowercase o. Then write your own.

Now trace O and o to finish the sentence.

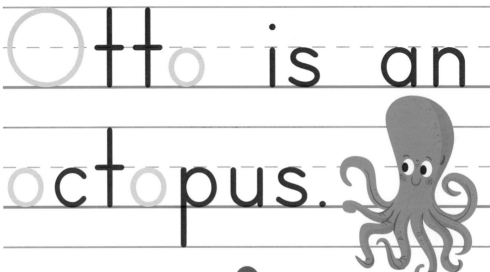

Otto is an octopus.

Oodles of Onions

Find and circle the **8** objects that start with the letter o in this Hidden Pictures puzzle.

octagon · oil can · octopus · olive · owl · orange · oboe · oar

Pp

This is an uppercase **P**.
This is a lowercase **p**.

Trace the uppercase **P**. Then write your own.

Trace the lowercase **p**. Then write your own.

Now trace **P** and **p** to finish the sentence.

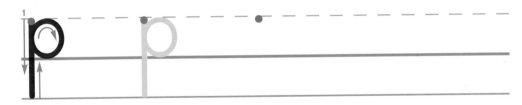

Poppy plays the piano.

P Is for Penguin!

Cross out the penguin that is different in each row.

What is your favorite thing to do in the winter?

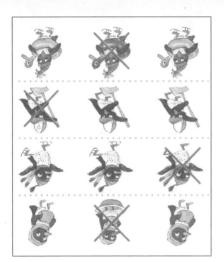

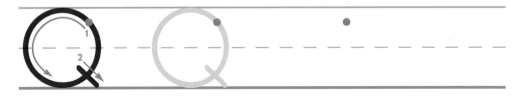

This is an uppercase Q.
This is a lowercase q.

Trace the uppercase Q. Then write your own.

Trace the lowercase q. Then write your own.

Now trace Q and q to finish the sentence.

Quinn is the

quickest quail.

75

The Queen's Quails

Circle the differences you see between these pictures.

One bird on this page is not a quail. Can you find it?

Rr
This is an uppercase **R**.
This is a lowercase **r**.

Trace the uppercase **R**. Then write your own.

R R

Trace the lowercase **r**. Then write your own.

r r

Now trace **R** and **r** to finish the sentence.

Ryan loves to read.

River Rafts

Find and circle the **8** objects that start with the letter **r** in this Hidden Pictures puzzle.

rolling pin   racket   rose   ring   ruler   rope   rake   rocket

Ss

This is an uppercase S.
This is a lowercase s.

Trace the uppercase S. Then write your own.

S S

Trace the lowercase s. Then write your own.

s s

Now trace S and s to finish the sentence.

Sam plays in
the sand.

S Is for Sock!

Each sock except I has an exact match. Circle the I sock with no match.

Can you think of 3 other words that start with the letter S?

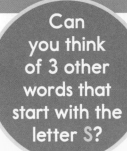

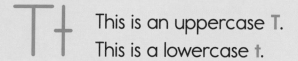

This is an uppercase T.
This is a lowercase t.

Trace the uppercase T. Then write your own.

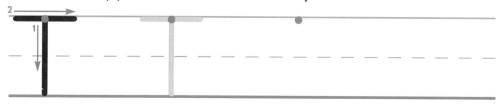

Trace the lowercase t. Then write your own.

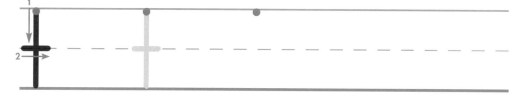

Now trace T and t to finish the sentence.

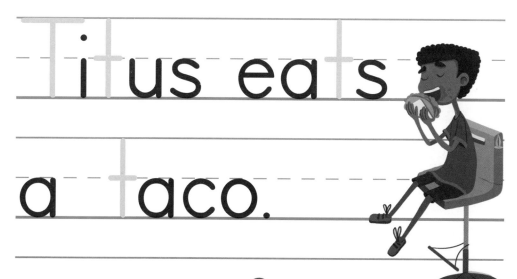

Titus eats a taco.

87

T Party

What else do you see that starts with the letter T?

Circle each T you see. How many did you find?

U u

This is an uppercase **U**.
This is a lowercase **u**.

Trace the uppercase **U**. Then write your own.

U U

Trace the lowercase **u**. Then write your own.

u u

Now trace **U** and **u** to finish the sentence.

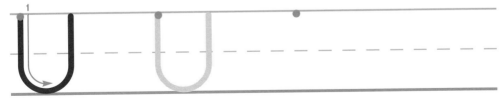

Uma uses an

umbrella.

Undercover U's

Use yellow to color in each space with the letter U. Use **blue** to color the other letters. What do you see?

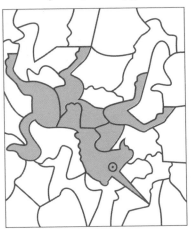

It's a unicorn!

Vv

This is an uppercase V.
This is a lowercase v.

Trace the uppercase V. Then write your own.

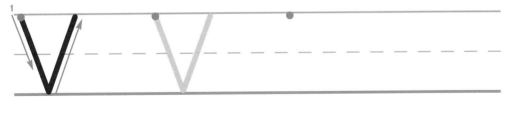

Trace the lowercase v. Then write your own.

Now trace V and v to finish the sentence.

Viv drives

a van.

V Is for Valentine!

Can you find 10 hearts at this Valentine's Day party? Color the valentines below as you find each one.

Ww

This is an uppercase **W**.
This is a lowercase **w**.

Trace the uppercase **W**. Then write your own.

Trace the lowercase **w**. Then write your own.

Now trace **W** and **w** to finish the sentence.

Wanda has
a watch.

Whale Watching

Find and circle the **8** objects that start with the letter **w** in this Hidden Pictures puzzle.

wagon wheel

waffle

whisk broom

wishbone

101

watermelon

whistle

watch

window

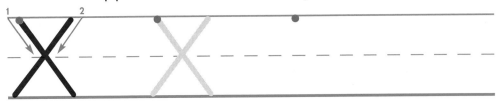

This is an uppercase **X**.
This is a lowercase **x**.

Trace the uppercase **X**. Then write your own.

X X X

Trace the lowercase **x**. Then write your own.

x x x

Now trace **X** to finish the sentence.

Xavier gets

an X-ray.

103

X Is for X-Ray!

Find and circle 6 differences between these X-rays.

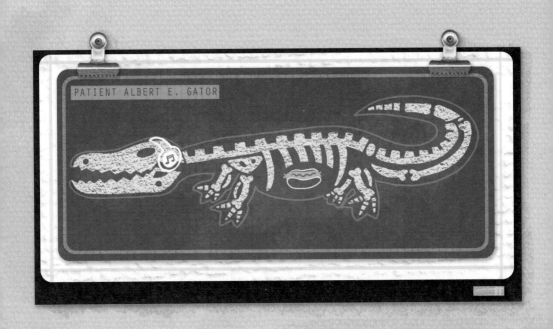

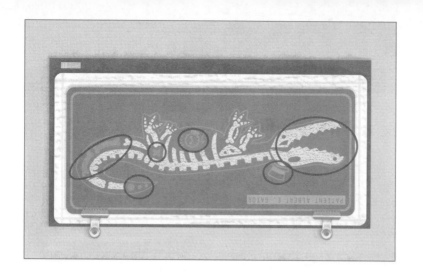

This is an uppercase Y.
This is a lowercase y.

Trace the uppercase Y. Then write your own.

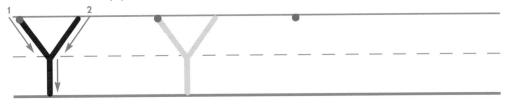

Trace the lowercase y. Then write your own.

Now trace Y and y to finish the sentence.

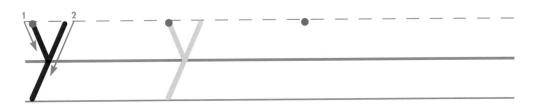

Yellow yaks
say hi.

Yak Snack

Circle each Y you see. How many did you find?

Can you think of another word that starts with the letter Y?

Zz

This is an uppercase **Z**.
This is a lowercase **z**.

Trace the uppercase **Z**. Then write your own.

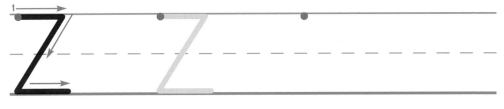

Trace the lowercase **z**. Then write your own.

Now trace **Z** and **z** to finish the sentence.

Zuzu zooms

past.

Z Is for Zebra!

What is Zak trying on? Connect the dots from 1 to 13 to find out.

What can you find on a coat that begins with the letter Z and rhymes with the word *flipper*?

Letter Match

Cut out each lowercase letter. Then paste it next to its uppercase match.

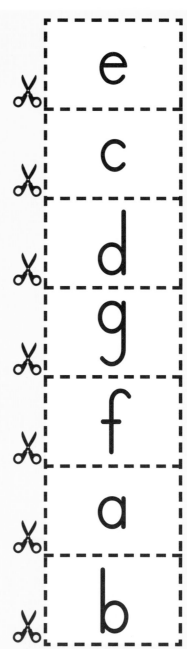

Letter Match

Cut out each lowercase letter. Then paste it next to its uppercase match.

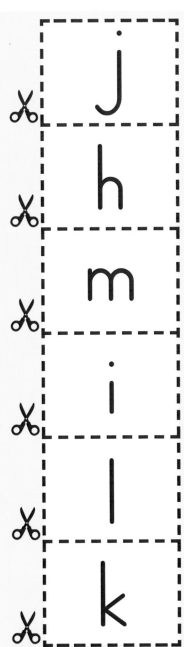

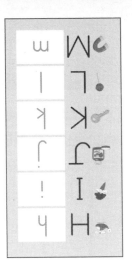

Letter Match

Cut out each lowercase letter. Then paste it next to its uppercase match.

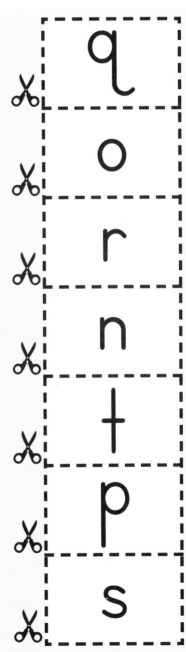

Letter Match

Cut out each lowercase letter. Then paste it next to its uppercase match.

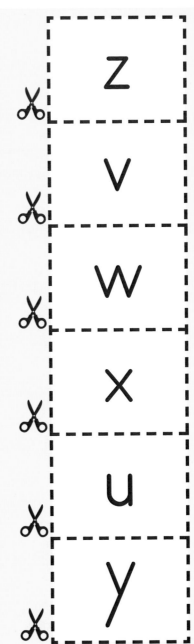

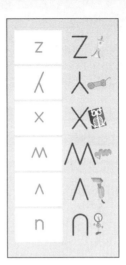

ABC Order

Fill in the missing uppercase letters
to help Herman reach his new shell.

A ☐ C D ☐

J ☐ H G F

K ☐ M N ☐ P

☐ T ☐ R Q

V W ☐ Y Z

abc Order

Fill in the missing lowercase letters to help Ava reach her friend Zippy.

125

Animal Opposites

Cut out each picture at the bottom of the page. Then paste each one beneath its opposite.

If two things are opposite, they are totally different.

Big

Tall

Fast

Slow

Small

Short

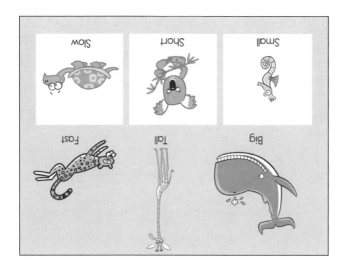

A Day of Opposites

Cut out each picture at the bottom of the page. Then paste each one beneath its opposite.

Inside

Dirty

Day

Clean

Night

Outside

✂

Outside

Clean

Night

Inside

Dirty

Day

Rhyme Time

Words that rhyme have the same ending sounds. Say the names of the pictures in each row. Circle the **2** that rhyme.

cat   hat   dog

clock   cake   snake

log   cow   frog

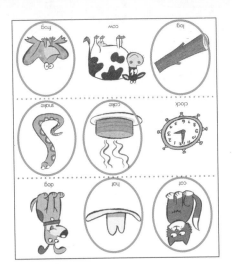

More Rhyme Time

Rhyming words are words that end with the same sound.

Say the name of each object. Cut out the pictures on the right. Paste each one next to the object that rhymes with it.

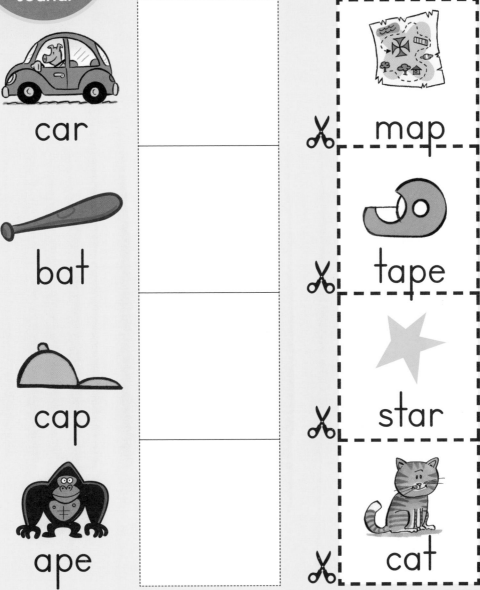

car

bat

cap

ape

map

tape

star

cat

Ship Shape

Cut out the **8** shapes at the bottom of the page. Then paste each one into its correct space above.

circle ◯

square ☐

triangle △

rectangle ▭

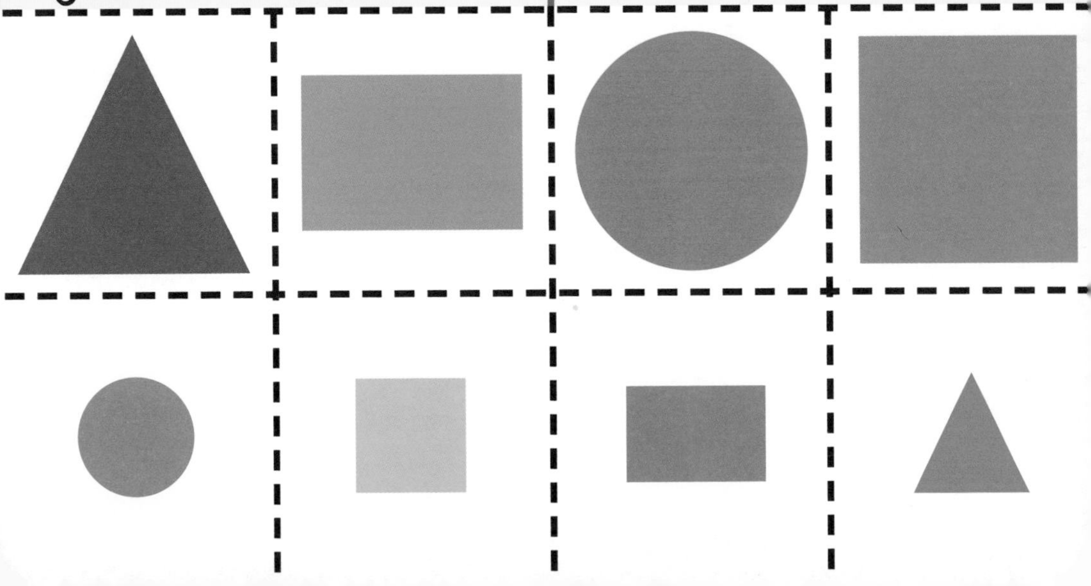

Shape Up

Trace each shape word. Say it out loud. Then draw a line to match it with its shape.

circle

triangle

square

rectangle

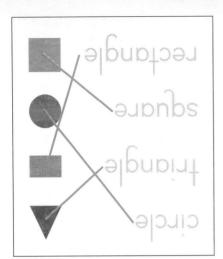

Sort the Sea Stars

Help sort these sea stars. Draw a line from each one to the pail with the same color.

Which pail will have the most sea stars?

PURPLE   YELLOW   RED

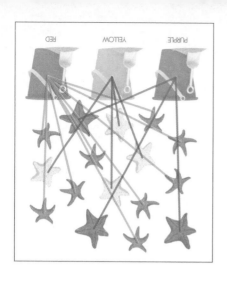

Which pail will have
the most sea stars?
THE RED PAIL

Write in Color

Trace each color word. Say it out loud. Then draw a line from each word to the paint that matches it.

yellow

purple

green

orange

red

blue

141

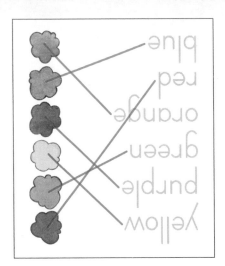

Wild or Farm?

Say the name of each animal below. Some are farm animals and some are wild animals. Cut each one out. Then paste it where it belongs.

farm | wild

lion

bear

pig

zebra

sheep

cow

Animal Round-Up

Trace each animal word. Say it out loud. Then draw a line to match it with its animal.

lion

pig

cow

sheep

zebra

bear

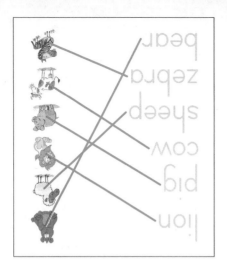

bear

zebra

sheep

cow

pig

lion

What Doesn't Belong

Cross out the thing in each row that doesn't belong. Tell why the other things go together.

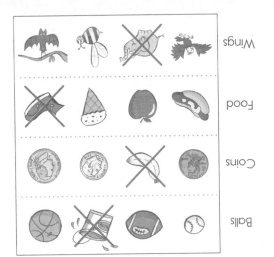

Wings

Food

Coins

Balls

What's Different?

Circle all the differences you see between these pictures. Can you find at least 10?

What would you pack on a picnic?

149

How Would You Feel?

Cut out the emojis at the bottom of the page. Paste one onto each scene to show how you would feel.

How Do You Feel?

Draw a picture to show how you are feeling right now.
Then write or tell about your picture.

I am feeling . . .

_____

_ _ _ _ _ _ _ _ _ _ _ _ _ _ _ _ _

_____

Yummy!

What is your favorite food? Draw a picture of it here.
Then tell or write why you like it.

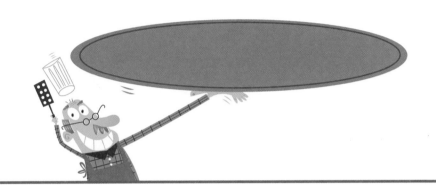

I like . . .

_____

- - - - - - - - - - - - - - - - -

_____

because . . .

_____

- - - - - - - - - - - - - - - - -

_____

Mouse Mail

These pictures are all mixed up. Cut out the pictures. Then paste them in the correct order to show how Mimi mailed a letter.

Use the pasted pictures to tell a story!

1	2	3

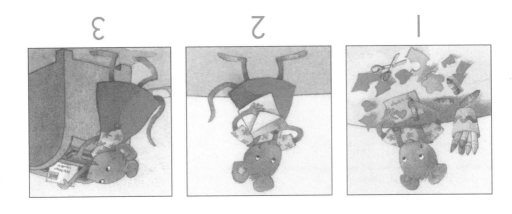

Mouse Munch

These pictures are all mixed up. Cut out the pictures. Then paste them in the correct order to show how Mimi packed her lunch.

Use the pasted pictures to tell a story!

1	2	3

Owl Puppets

Cut out each of the owls on this page and the next. Give them each a name. Then see page 165.

Owl Puppets

Cut out each of the owls on this page. Give them each a name. Then see page 165.

A Stick-Puppet Show!

Cut out the **6** owls on pages 161 and 163. Then tape a craft stick, chenille stick, or drinking straw to the back of each owl. You'll have your own set of puppets!

Use your puppets to put on a show for your family. You can make up stories for your puppets. Here are a few ideas to get you started:

- It was the first day of school and . . .
- Otto was ready for bed when . . .
- Let's go to the park!

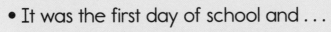

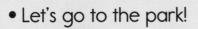

BONUS!
Find the 2 finger puppets below that look the same.

What's Your Story?

Think about something fun you did this week. Draw pictures to show what you did. Tell or write about it.

First I . . .

Then I . . .

At the end, I felt . . .

How's the Weather?

Cut out the **3** kids. Then paste each into the correct scene. Look at their clothing for clues where each one should go.

Use the photos to tell about the weather in each scene.

Help the Helpers!

These community helpers need your help. Cut out each item. Then paste each item with the correct person.

Use the photos to tell about each helper.

doctor

carpenter

crossing guard

firefighter

hose

hammer

stethoscope

stop sign

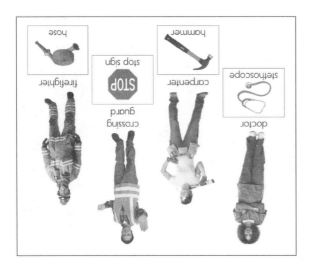

firefighter

hose

crossing
guard

stop sign

carpenter

hammer

doctor

stethoscope

Animal Match

Cut out the baby animals at the bottom of the page.
Paste each one next to its parent.

Use the photos to tell about the animal parents and their babies.

cow

chicken

horse

pig

✂

chick

✂

piglet

✂

foal

✂

calf

cow

calf

chicken

chick

horse

pig

piglet

foal

Pet Portrait

Think about a pet you have or would like to have. Draw a picture of it here. Then tell or write about it.

This pet is a _____.

It looks _____

because it has _____.

When it moves, it _____.

Investigate:
Finger Fun!

YOU NEED:

• shaving cream • shallow pan

1. Put some shaving cream in the pan.

2. Use your fingers to make designs. Make the letters in your name. Say the letters out loud as you make them. Then draw the number that shows how old you are.

TALK ABOUT IT!

• How does the shaving cream look, feel, and smell?

• How can you use it to make shapes? What shapes will you make?

Investigate more: Color It!

YOU NEED:
- shaving cream
- 3 bowls
- red, yellow, and blue food coloring

Red, yellow, and blue are primary colors. You can mix 2 of them to make secondary colors. Green, orange, and purple are secondary colors.

1. Put some shaving cream in each bowl.
2. Add 2 drops of blue and yellow coloring to one bowl.
3. Repeat with yellow and red coloring. Then try with red and blue.

What happens when you mix the colors? Color the chart.

When I mix these two colors . . .				I get this color:
blue	+	yellow	=	
yellow	+	red	=	
red	+	blue	=	

TALK ABOUT IT!

- What did you find out?
- How could you change the colors that you mixed?
- Think about mixing blue, yellow, and red. What color might that make? How could you test your ideas?

Investigate:
Sink or Float?

YOU NEED:
- a large bowl of water
- objects, such as: eraser, coin, fruit, paperclip, crayon, rubber band, pebble, paint brush, etc.

An object **sinks when it** goes to the bottom of the water. An object **floats** when it stays on top of the water.

1. Look at each object. Make a prediction. Will it sink or float? Why or why not?

2. Test your predictions. Drop each object into the water.

TALK ABOUT IT!
- Were your predictions correct?
- Did anything float for a while and then sink?
- What surprised you?

🔍 Investigate more: Sort It!

Look at each object below. Circle the ones you think would float. Draw an X over the ones you think would sink. Then test your predictions with these objects or similar ones you find around the house.

TALK ABOUT IT!
- Why do you think some objects sink?
- Why do you think some objects float?

How would you build a boat that could help the sinking objects to float?

Investigate:
Look at Shadows

Go outside. Can you see your shadow?
What is it shaped like?

Look at this girl's shadow.
Her shadow is shaped like
her. Why do shadows form?

Do shadows always look
the same? Why or why not?

Draw lines to match these shadows with the objects that
made them.

Investigate more: Shadow Puppets

YOU NEED:
- craft sticks • foam shapes • clear tape
- flashlight or adjustable reading lamp

1. Place a craft stick on a foam shape. Use clear tape to attach the shape to the stick.
2. Pull down the shades and shine the flashlight or reading lamp onto a blank wall.
3. Hold your puppets between the light source and the wall and make the puppets move!

TALK ABOUT IT!

- Move a puppet closer to the light. How does the shadow change?
- Move the puppet farther away. What happens? Why?

Investigate:
Birdsong Bonanza

Songbirds fly from tree to tree,
each singing its own melody.
Robin chirps, *Cheer up! Cheerily.*
Goldfinch calls, *Per-chick-o-ree!*
Bluebird cheeps, *Tu-a-wee! Tu-a-wee!*
Chickadee chants, *Chick-a-dee-dee-dee!*

Bird sounds
send messages.
Some sounds mean
"Danger." Some mean
"Stay out." Others
mean "I'm looking
for a mate."

Now it's your turn.
Think of sounds you can make with
your body, such as clapping, stomping,
and humming. If you wanted to send a
message to people without using words,
what would it sound like? Create your own
"people-song" and share it with your family.
See if they can guess what message you
are sending.

💡 Invent:
Bird's Nest Challenge

Look at these nests. What are they made of? How do you think birds made them?

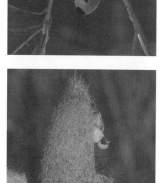

Now it's your turn. Design a nest. Use only things from your yard or a nearby park.

1. Go outside. Gather materials for your nest.

2. Make a plan. Draw a picture that shows your nest design.

3. Follow your plan to make a nest. Share your nest with an adult. Tell how the nest would keep eggs and young birds safe.

TALK ABOUT IT!
Many birds make nests. Why do you think they do this?

Investigate:
Be an Explorer

YOU NEED:

- scissors - string or yarn - pad of drawing paper
- pencil - hand lens

1. Cut a long piece of string or yarn. Tie the ends together to make a large circle.

2. Put your circle on the ground in your yard or a nearby park. Use the hand lens to look at what is inside the circle. Draw what you see.

There's a little world in a small space!

Investigate more:
In the Little Worlds

A squirrel is a **living** thing. All living things:
- need food, water, and air.
- can grow.
- can make more living things like themselves.

A rock is a **non-living** thing. All non-living things:
- do not need food, water, and air.
- cannot grow.
- cannot make more things like themselves.

Look at the pictures below. Circle the living things. Draw an X on the non-living things.

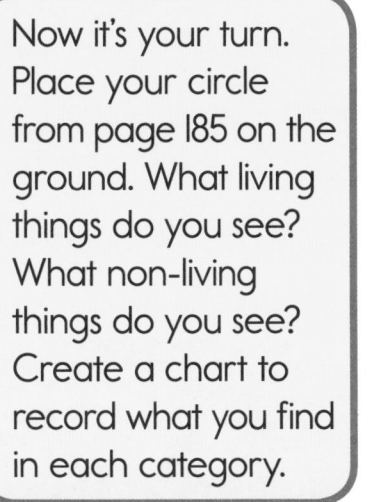

Now it's your turn. Place your circle from page 185 on the ground. What living things do you see? What non-living things do you see? Create a chart to record what you find in each category.

Investigate:
See the Water Move

YOU NEED:

• wax paper • toothpick • paper towel

1. Sprinkle water on wax paper.
2. Use a toothpick to move the drops of water. What happens when the drops touch?
3. Try this again on a paper towel. Can you move the water? What happens to the paper towel?

What happens with water on different materials?

TALK ABOUT IT!

• What happens to water on wax paper? Why?
• What happens to water on a paper towel? Why?
• Think of another material. What do you think water would do on that material? Why do you think so?

Invent: Water Testing

What happens with water on each material? Draw lines to match. Then use the pictures to talk about what happens and why.

Now it's your turn. Think about what happens with water on different materials.

1. Find 2 materials to test. Choose something that you think will absorb, or soak up, water and something that you think will not absorb water.

2. Plan a test.

3. Test each material.

4. What did you find out? Did one of the materials absorb water? Did one repel it? Why?

Investigate: Hiding in Plain Sight

This animal is a baby tapir. It is born with spots and stripes. The spots and stripes look like shadows in the rain forest. This makes the baby tapir hard to see. Being hard to see helps keep it safe.

Go for a walk outside. Look for animals. Think about how their feathers or fur help them blend into their surroundings.

Colors, patterns, and other features that help an animal blend in with its surroundings are called camouflage.

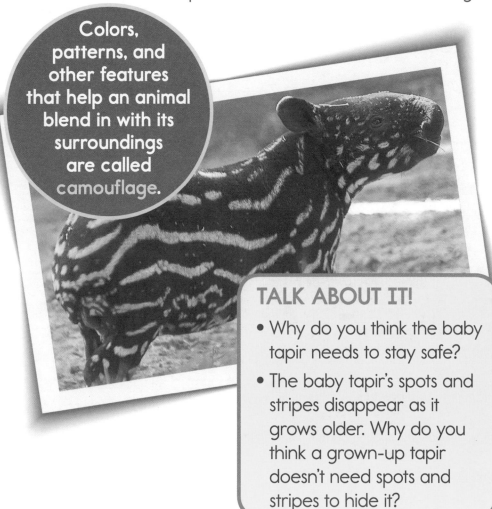

TALK ABOUT IT!

- Why do you think the baby tapir needs to stay safe?
- The baby tapir's spots and stripes disappear as it grows older. Why do you think a grown-up tapir doesn't need spots and stripes to hide it?

Invent: Your Own Animal

Invent and draw an animal that could blend in with the surroundings in this picture. Give your animal colors that help it blend in. Think about adding a pattern, such as spots or stripes. How might its shape help it blend in?

Some animals have colors that help them blend in with gray or brown stones or trees. Animals in places with green leaves and lots of flowers may blend in even if they're brightly colored.

TALK ABOUT IT!

- What do you see in the picture?
- Tell how your animal's body helps it blend in.
- How would you dress if you wanted to blend in with the picture?

Investigate:
Sorting Out Rocks

1. Collect some rocks.

2. Spread them out so you can see them all.

3. Sort the rocks in different ways, such as by color or shape. Are some rocks smooth and others rough? Are some rocks shiny and others dull?

4. Dab water on the rocks. How do they change?

TALK ABOUT IT!

- What are some ways you sorted your rocks?

- What do you notice about your rocks?

- How can you find out what kind of rocks you have?

Investigate:
Water Power

1. Get a handful of dirt.
2. Pour water on it. What happened?
3. Now gather some rocks. Which look like they have been worn down by water?

Over time, moving water wears down rock just like it makes paths in dirt. The water eats away at the rocks and makes their edges smooth. It is a very powerful force!

Circle the rocks that you think have been worn down by water. What about those rocks helped you decide?